THE BEST CAT BOOK EVER

KATE FUNK

ST. MARTIN'S GRIFFIN ≈ NEW YORK

THE BEST CAT BOOK EVER. Copyright © 2014 by Kate Funk.
All rights reserved. Printed in China. For information, address
St. Martin's Press, 175 Fifth Avenue, New York, N.Y. 10010.

www.stmartins.com

Designed by Anna Gorovoy

Library of Congress Cataloging-in-Publication Data

Funk, Kate.
    The best cat book ever / Kate Funk.—First edition.
        p. cm.
    ISBN 978-1-250-05038-0 (paper over board)
    ISBN 978-1-4668-5148-1 (e-book)
 1. Cats. 2. Cats—Pictorial works. I. Title.
    SF446.F845 2014
    636.80022′2—dc23

                                                2014015995

St. Martin's Griffin books may be purchased for educational,
business, or promotional use. For information on bulk pur-
chases, please contact Macmillan Corporate and Premium
Sales Department at 1-800-221-7945, extension 5442, or
write specialmarkets@macmillan.com.

First Edition: November 2014

10 9 8 7 6 5 4 3 2 1

INTRODUCTION

EVER SINCE I WAS A LITTLE GIRL I DREAMED of having my own kitty. Instead, I had to settle for a room filled with cat figurines, stuffed cats, and pictures of kittens pasted all over my walls. Even when I moved away from home I always seemed to live either with a roommate who was allergic or in a place that didn't allow pets. In 2006, I moved in with my friend Brennan. He had a cat named Kitty, and we lived in an apartment with landlords who worked at a local humane society, so naturally they loved pets. Finally! I was able to find the kitty I had always dreamed of.

I knew I wanted a black cat from the get-go—there's just something about them I adore. So I did some research and finally found a no-kill shelter near me that had a black kitten up for adoption. I went to go check him out, but it turned out that, sadly, he was already spoken for. They told me they did have one other black kitten that had just come in, found abandoned and motherless. He was too little to leave just yet, and had some medical issues that needed to be taken care of first, but I could meet him if I wanted to. They put me in this tiny room with him and all of his siblings, so I could play with all of them first to make sure he was really the one I wanted. I sat down on a chair in the middle of the room and stared at all of these happy, crazy kittens playing with each other right in front of me. CUTEST THING EVER. This black kitten just stood in the corner of the room and stared at me, refusing to play with the rest. I reached over to see if he was okay with me petting him. He was, but he still just sat there and didn't join

in on the fun. He reminded me a lot of myself: a loner, and a bit of a weirdo. When it was time to go, they put all the kittens back in their cage and asked me which one I wanted to adopt. I thought about taking one of the playful, fun kittens home, but couldn't get the adorable black one out of my mind. He seemed so different from the rest. I was in love.

AC stands for "Annoying Customer," which comes from a scene in one of my favorite movies, *Clerks.* There was the unfortunate time when I told a customer that AC's name was Annoying Customer. She thought I was making a joke about her, and stormed

off in anger. So I had to shorten his name to AC. He's the most amazing little weirdo that I've ever met. While most of his days are spent sleeping in whatever room I happen to be working in (which I'm convinced is an evil plot to get me to take naps with him), he still seems to find time to stare at walls from an inch away, attempt to eat anything that isn't edible, and force me to carry him around like a baby (but then pretend he hates it if my husband comes into the room and sees him being a mama's boy).

Around the time that I got AC, I worked at a local paper store here in Milwaukee called Broadway Paper. One day we were making paper party hats, and I decided to make a tiny one to give to AC when I got home. To my shock, when I brought it home and put it on his head, he didn't seem to mind. He just walked around the house with it on like the awesome cat he is.

I have this friend who often calls AC a jerk. (Most people find AC's personality a bit off-putting since he doesn't really care for anyone except for me, and he always looks like he wants to kill you.) Her birthday was coming up, so I decided I would try and make her a birthday card featuring the "jerk cat" she loves so much. I made a little cake out of paper and threw together a messy backdrop made with construction paper, glue sticks, and a scissors, and topped it off with AC wearing the party hat I had made him. I was so excited with the result! His look of disdain contrasted perfectly with the bright happy birthday decorations. I liked it so much that I started printing more

copies to give to my other friends—including a fellow friend and employee of Broadway Paper. It was there that the owner saw this card and was intrigued. She asked if I had any more designs. I didn't, but told her I'd be more than happy to make some. I went home elated and came up with another five cards, had a meeting with the owner, and my greeting cards started to be carried and sold in my very first store.

From there things seemed to snowball. I partnered up with my roommate, Brennan, to make The World's Most Super Amazing 100% Awesome Cat Calendar. I took the photographs and he did the graphic design work. I attended my very first craft fair ever that same year: the Renegade Craft Fair in Chicago. It was amazing to see other people enjoy and admire my work, and to meet fellow artists like myself, who I had no idea were out there. I knew I'd found my people, so I continued to make more designs, get my products into more stores, and attend more craft fairs around the country. After five amazing years of hard work, I finally was able to quit my day job and devote my life to my dream occupation: Cat Photographer.

One of the biggest questions that I get from people is "How do I get AC to pose for these photos?"

Despite what some people may think, AC is actually dressed in the costumes and sitting in the dioramas I've created for each and every photograph . . . and he is a willing model at that (well . . . most of the time). There are some days he just isn't in the mood to pose. If that's the case and I can tell he isn't happy, we stop, wait until the next day, and hope he's in a better mood by then. Over the years I've slowly learned what he is and isn't willing to do and used that to my advantage. Having his favorite toy and a can of wet cat food nearby to distract him between shots doesn't hurt either.

A lot of preparation goes into each shoot. After some hardcore brainstorming, I sketch out an idea (and make sure there is actually a way to execute it that AC will also agree on). Then I'll spend a good week painting the backgrounds, making any props needed, and sewing AC's outfits. Even setting up and lighting a scene on shoot day can take up to an hour. AC always comes out to investigate during this part, which I find strange. Never once has it occurred to him to run and hide. After all this time and preparation, it comes down to a matter of a couple of minutes to try and shoot the photograph. And as much as I can plan an idea in my head, I never actually know how it's going to turn out in the end. But that's my favorite part: seeing the final result and sharing that result with everyone else and hoping they find as much joy in it as I do.

I sat in my booth at a craft show recently and watched little girl after girl walk past my booth and squeal with excitement when they'd see the pillows I'd made with AC dressed as a unicorn on them. It made me think back to little Kate Funk and her room filled with cat decorations and her dreams of own-ing her own kitty someday. I think she'd be pretty pumped if I could tell her how her life turned out.

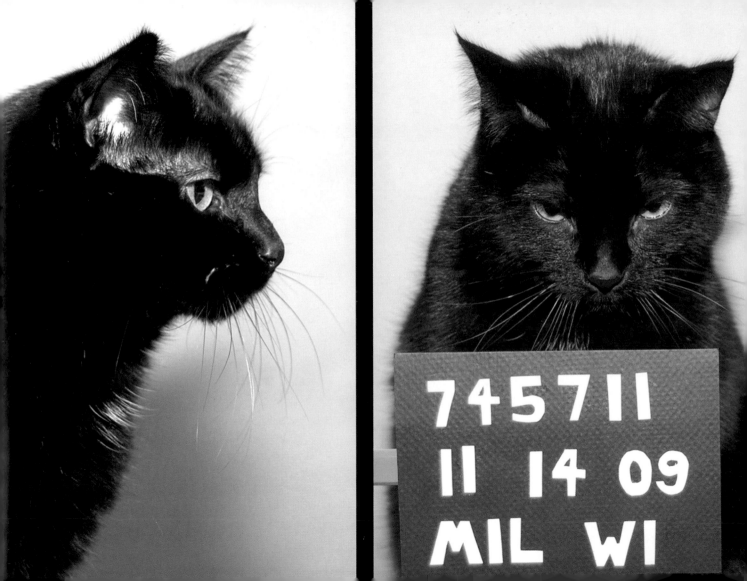

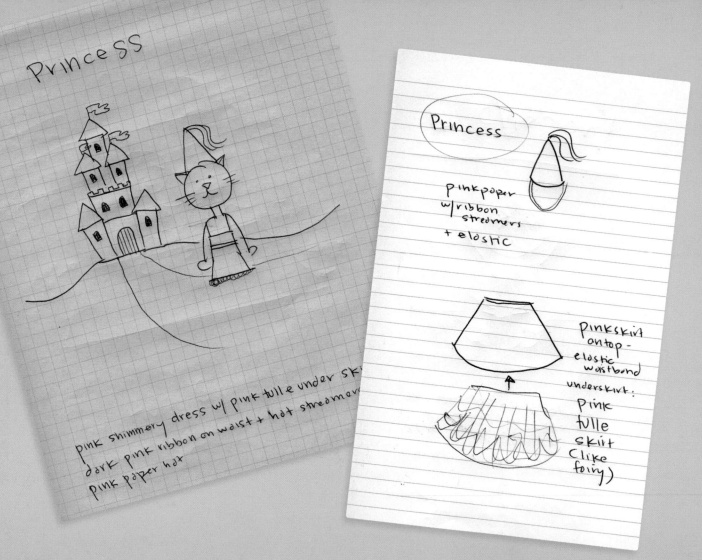

Princess

pink shimmery dress w/ pink tulle under ski[rt]
dark pink ribbon on waist + hot streamer[s]
pink paper hat

Princess

pinkpaper
w/ribbon
streamers
+ elastic

pinkskirt
ontop -
elastic
waistband

underskirt:
pink
tulle
skirt
(like
fairy)

make mushrooms
out of felt this time?

use real pink/showy
flamingo

astro turf

white fence

nice
flowers
(tulips)   mushrooms

pink
flamingo

red h__

← blue shi__
black belt
gold buckle

greenroom®

LUchador!

make costume blue +
gold - cape gold inside
and blue outside
cardboard in collar

background - red stripes

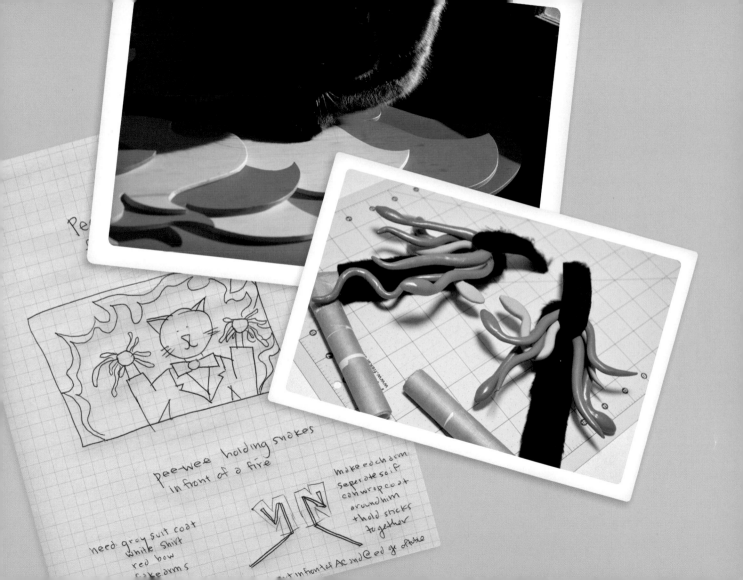

pee-wee holding snakes
in front of a fire

make red charm
seperate so if
can wrap coat
around him
+ hold sticks
together

need gray suit coat
white shirt
red bow
cake arms

_t infront of AC md@ ge of place

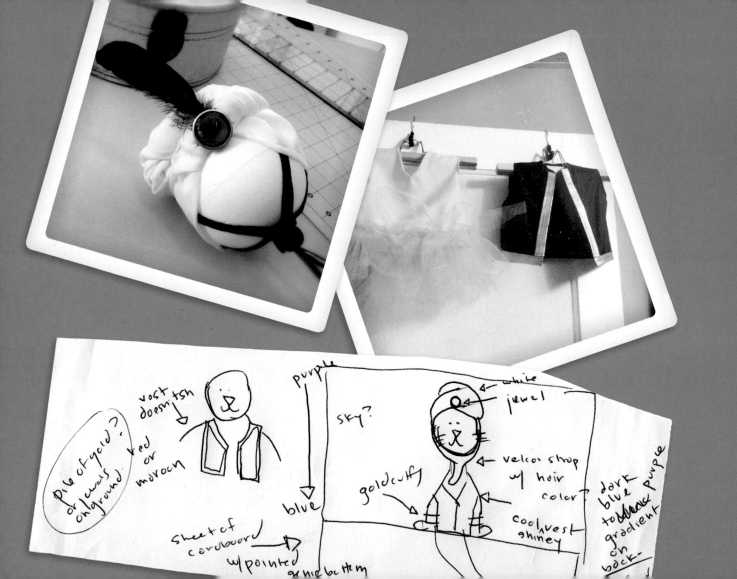

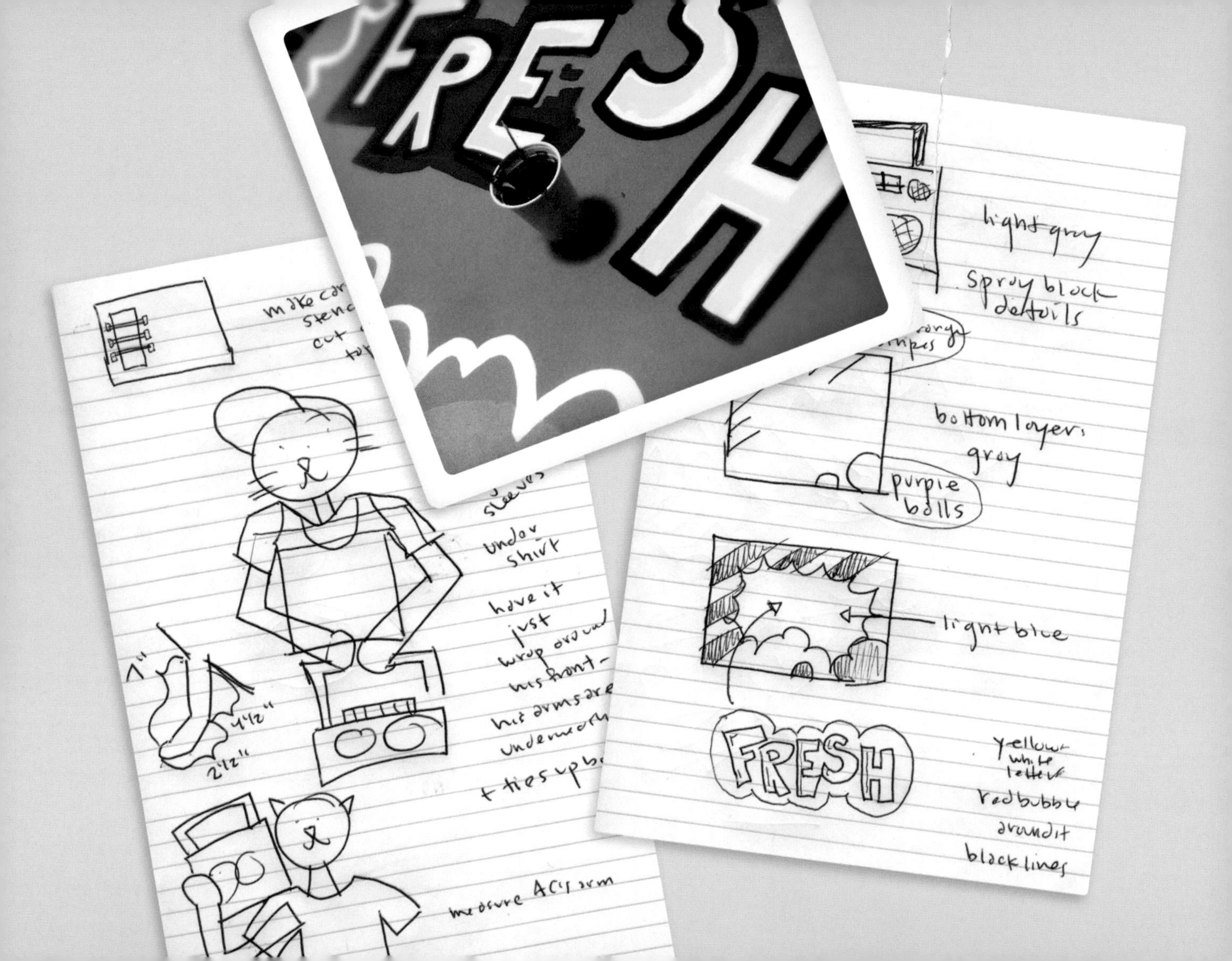

FRESH
light gray
spray block details
bottom layers gray
purple balls
light blue
FRESH
yellow white letters
red bubble around it
black lines
sleeves
under shirt
have it just wrap around his front -
his arms are
measure AC's arm

littlered riding hood

wolf silhouette?
white floor for snow — snow
                        falling

all black, white + grey background
AC in red cape!

background grey sky w/ white
clouds like Zeus

Glamour Shots!!!

· solid background

· backlight to get outer glow on hair

· add vaseline effect

hot pinks or purples or reds

super glittery jewelry

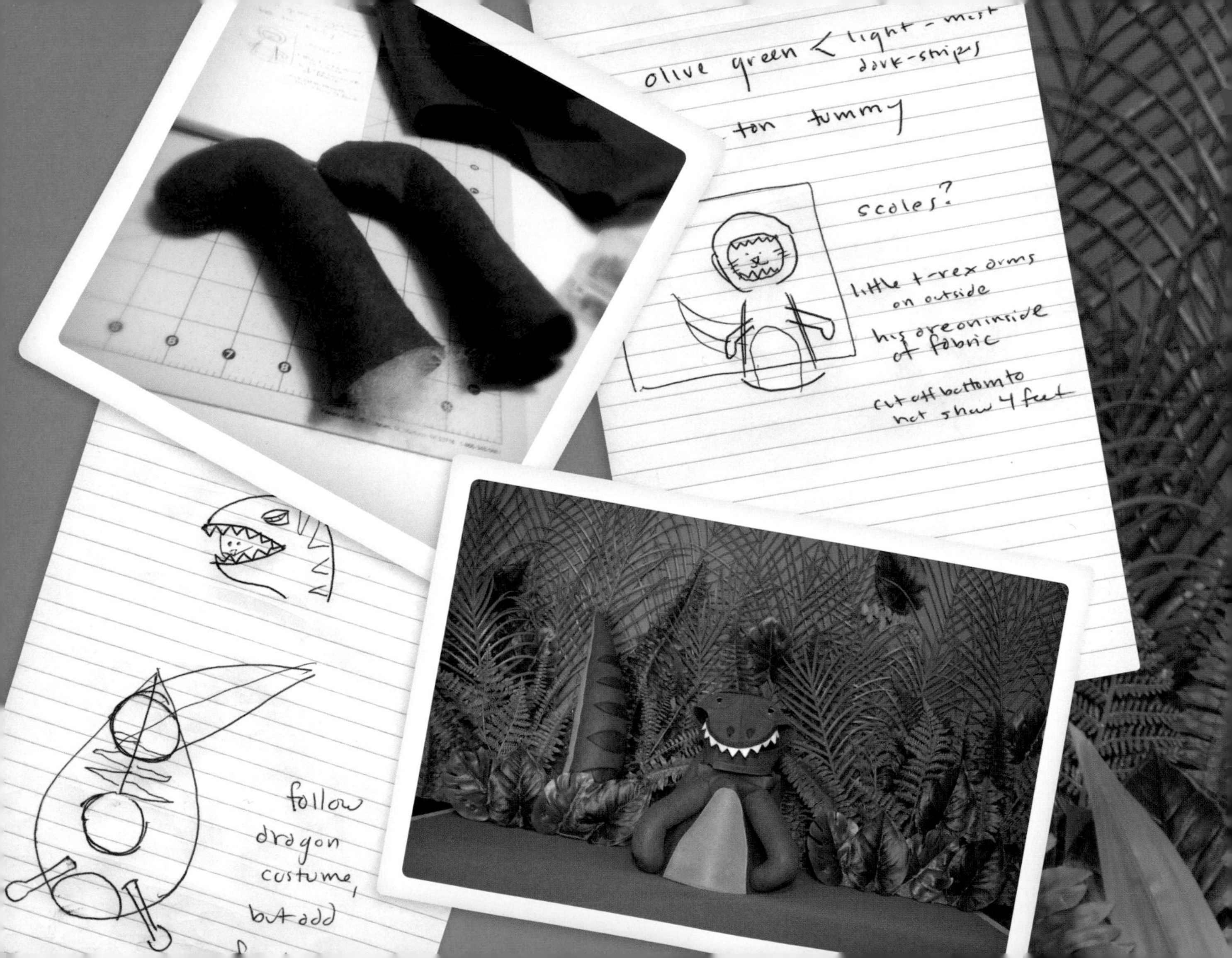

olive green < light - mist
dark-stripes

ton tummy

scales?

little t-rex arms
on outside

his are on inside
of fabric

cut off bottom to
not show 4 feet

follow
dragon
costume,
but add

blue
sky

White
mountains
Spray
paint
w/glitter

North
Pole

greenroom®

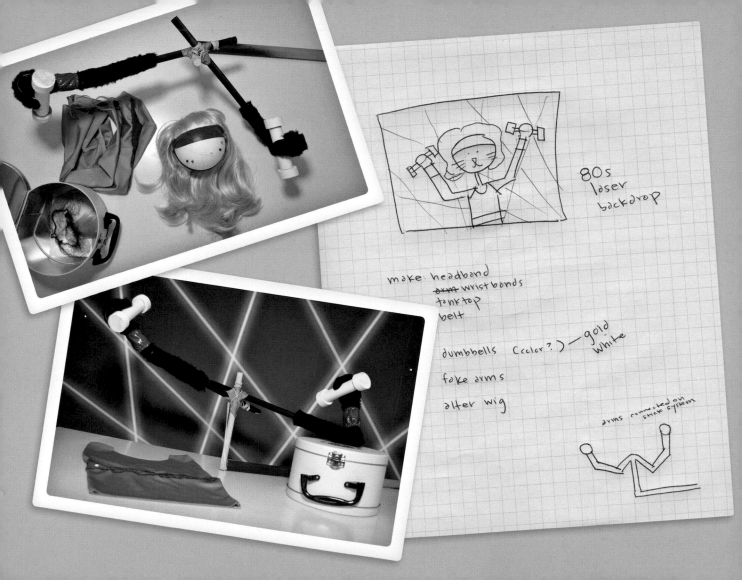

80s
laser
backdrop

make: headband
~~wrist~~ wristbands
tank top
belt

dumbbells (color?) — gold
white

fake arms

alter wig

arms connected on
stick system

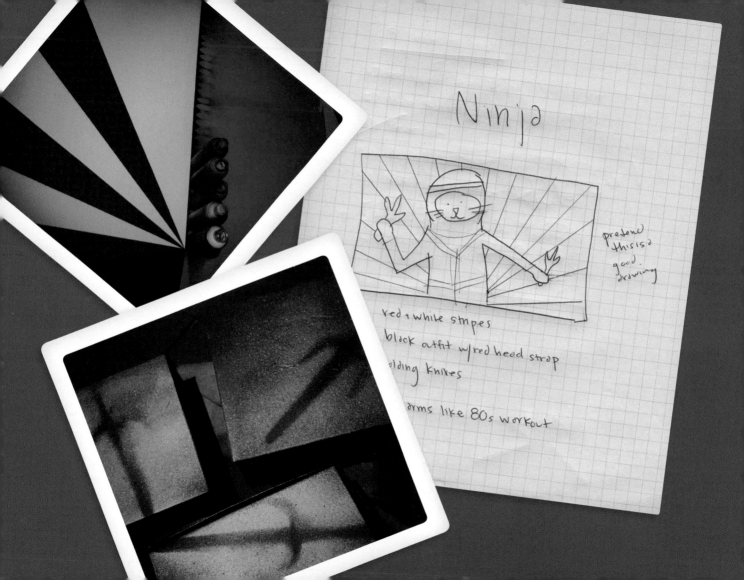

Ninja

pretend
this is a
good
drawing

red + white stripes

black outfit w/ red head strap

holding knives

arms like 80s workout

OWL

ears?

brown felt — whites+off white+tans
for tummy

make shape of t-rex cost[...]

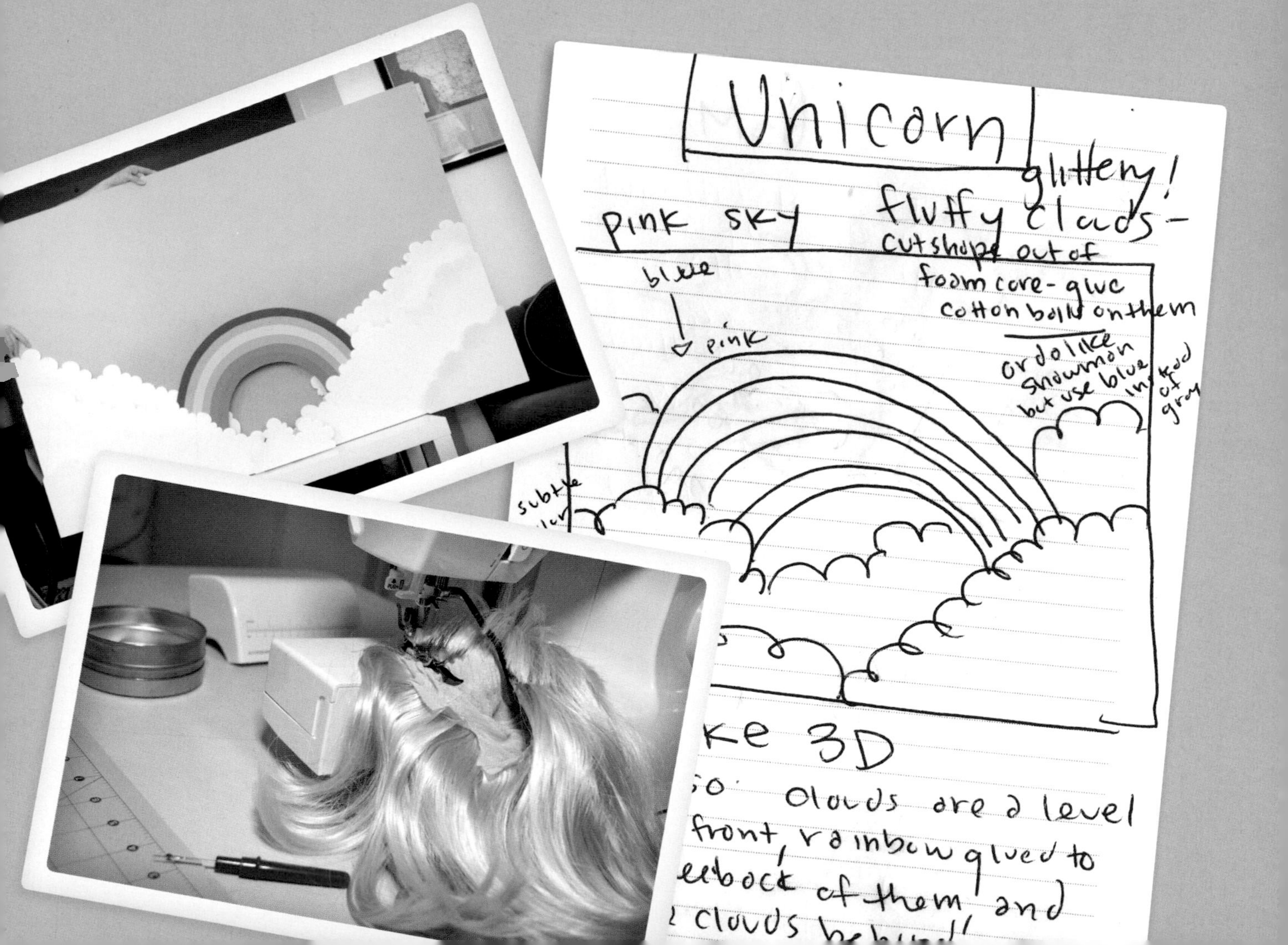

Unicorn

glittery!

pink sky

blue
→ pink

fluffy clouds —
cut shape out of
foam core - glue
cotton balls on them

or do like
snowman
but use blue
instead of
grey

subtle
color

...ke 3D

so. clouds are a level
front, rainbow glued to
...ee back of them and
...clouds behind!

mermaid bottom made of
felt w/ green r blue colors —
not actually attached. he
just leans into it

ACKNOWLEDGMENTS

THANK YOU FIRST AND FOREMOST TO ANNA, Laura C., Laura F., Michelle, and all the people over at St. Martin's Press for this amazing opportunity and all their hard work to make it happen. Thanks especially to Hannah for taking a chance on me and my crabby black cat.

Thank you to Eddie for all his help in guiding me along the way.

Thanks to my husband, Jay, for supporting my dreams to make this into my job, for all his help, and for being my cat wrangler. Without him most of these photographs wouldn't exist.

Thank you to Brennan for being my partner in this from the beginning, for his amazing work on the calendars every year, for all his advice, and for putting up with my endless, rambling emails.

Thank you to my family for all their love and support, especially to my parents for always giving me the opportunity to be who I am. I am beyond grateful for all your encouragement.

Thank you to Michael Patterson for shooting our amazing Kickstarter video that made all of this happen.

Thank you to all the AC fans out there who find humor and joy in what I do and made it possible for this to become my life.

And finally, thank you to AC for being 100% awesome. Who knew a cat considered to be bad luck would bring such love, friendship, and amazing opportunities into my life? I love you, dude.

Thank you to Tracie Stier-Johnson and the Renegade Craft Fair crew for being the first people to take a chance on me.

Thank you to Scott Bergmann for taking the time to help out and make me an amazing, cat-sized Bob Ross painting.